HUMAN SKULL COLORING PATTERNS

Stress relive patterns : 36 Different pattern of relieving stress

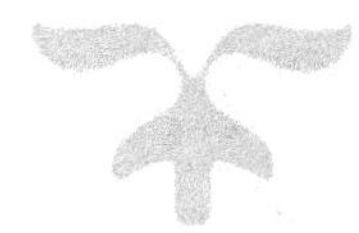

[DATE]
MICROSOFT
[Company address]

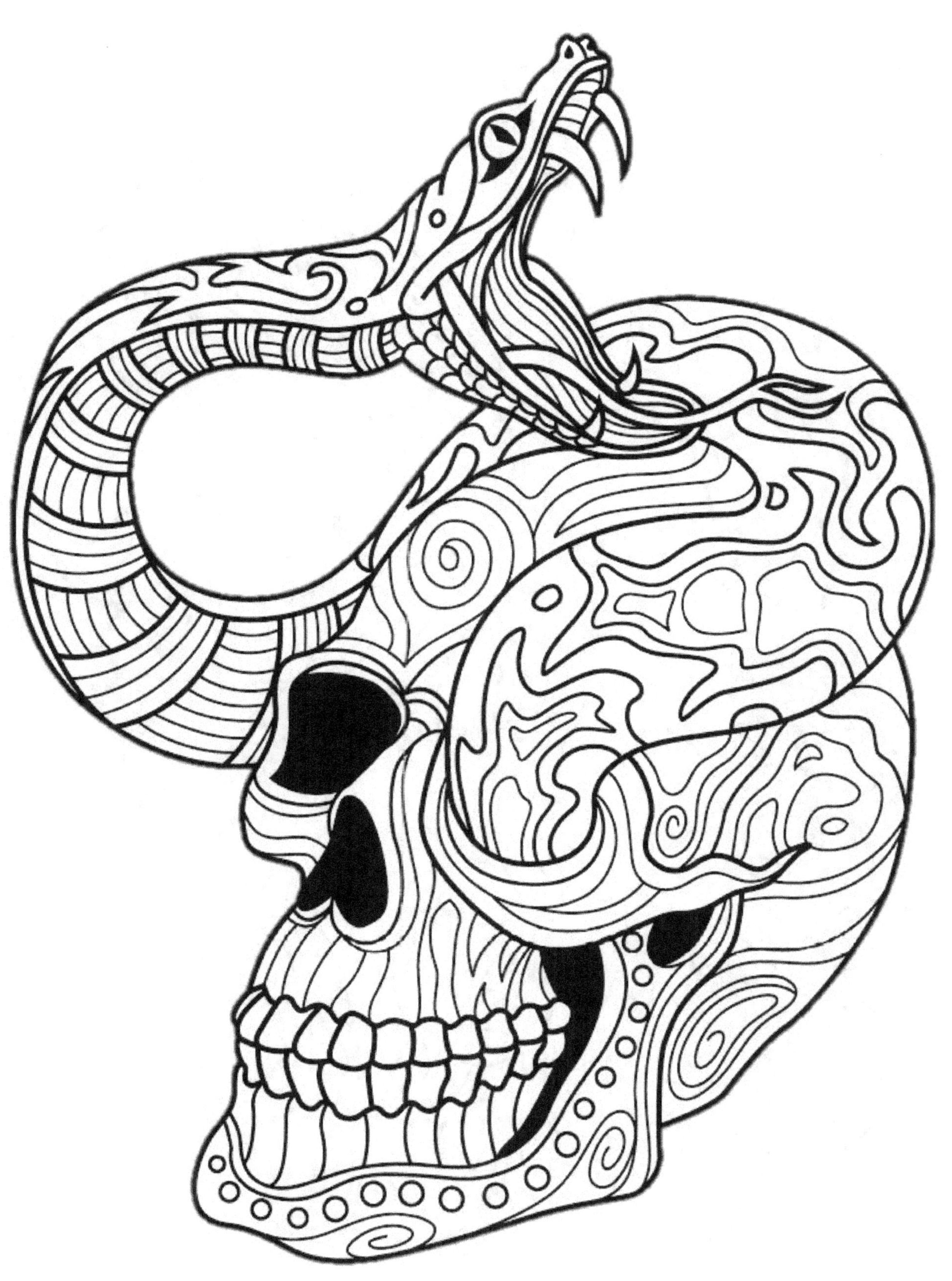

Recetas
OMP

a. Thomas 1/13

The Sands of Time

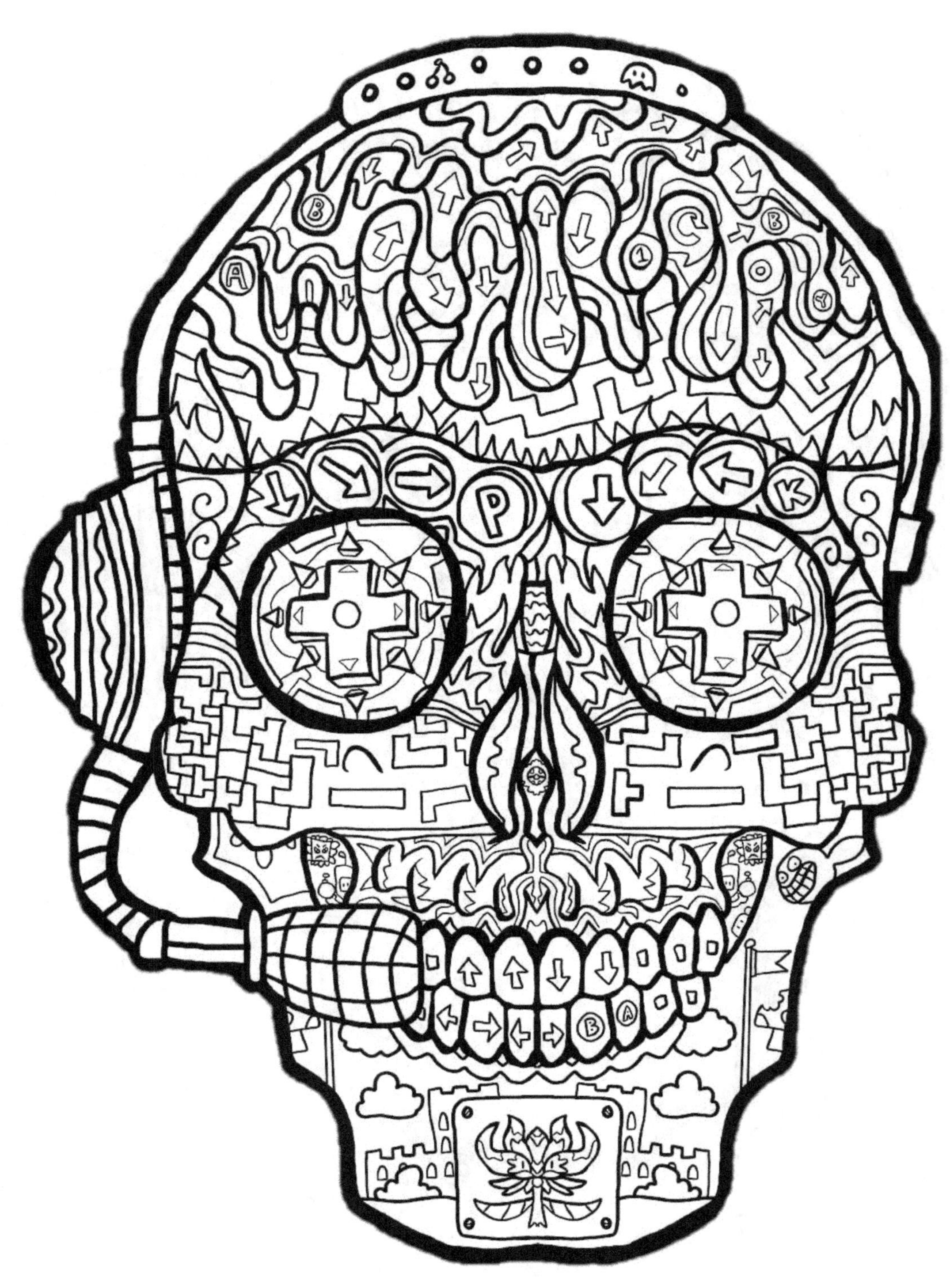

www.ingramcontent.com/pod-product-compliance
Lightning Source LLC
Chambersburg PA
CBHW081637250726
48657CB00009B/2927